Tab

INTRODUCTION

CHAPTER 1   LEARN THE BASICS

CHAPTER 2   BUILD YOUR OWN BUSINESS

CHAPTER 3   BINARY OPTIONS

CHAPTER 4   TRADER'S MINDSET

CHAPTER 5   OPTIONS "PUT" AND OPTIONS "CALL"

CHAPTER 6   THE MOST EFFECTIVE STRATEGIES

CHAPTER 7   OTHER STRATEGIES

CHAPTER 8   BULL AND BEAR CALL SPREAD

CHAPTER 9   CHOOSING A BROKER

CHAPTER 10   FINANCIAL LEVERAGE

CHAPTER 11   WHAT ARE "THE GREEKS"

CHAPTER 12   TIPS FOR BEGINNERS

CHAPTER 13   AVOIDING COMMON PITFALLS IN OPTIONS TRADING

CONCLUSION

Introduction

There is often confusion about why traders choose options when stocks and bonds do just fine. What some tend to miss out is the vast difference in the earnings potential. Stocks generally return a profit of 8% - 12% per annum, which is pretty impressive in and of it. However, options are a lot more lucrative with a much larger potential.

Some options trades typically generate profits upwards of 50%. Making 100% profits within a short period of time and even more, is not unheard of. This is why a lot of experienced traders choose options. They are extremely lucrative and highly profitable. It is also possible to make money trading options in any market condition. Traders can make money when the market is bullish, bearish, and even when it is stagnant. As such, you do not need specific market conditions, and hence profitability throughout the year is very possible.

Experts agree that trading options offer plenty of benefits that are not offered by other types of securities. While not all traders may want to engage in options trading, there are certain aspects of it that other traders find attractive.

Potential for Astronomical Profits

One of the main reasons for trading options is the opportunity of making significantly large profits compared to all other forms of trade in the markets. This is possible even without large sums of money. The principle behind this approach is leverage. A trader needs not to have large amounts of funds to earn huge profits. For instance, with as little as $10,000, it is possible to earn amounts such as $300,000 or even $800,000 simply by using leverage.

Take the example of a trader whose trading fund is $10,000. The trader wishes to invest this amount in Company ABC. Now the current stock price is $20 though this price is expected to rise. The trader could use the funds to directly purchase the shares and receive a total of 500 shares for his money. If the stock price was to rise to $25 within a month, the trader would have made $5 per share or a total of $2,500 in profits.

Alternatively, the trader could purchase call options of XYZ stocks with the same amount of money. The options allow the trader to purchase back the underlying stocks within a certain period of time. Now, options contracts cost between $1 and $4 depending on certain factors such as the value of the underlying security. In our example, one call options costs $2 so for the $10,000, the trader receives 5,000 options contracts.

If the trader chooses to exercise the right to sell the underlying shares in the next month, then he stands to make a profit of $5 per share. Remember that he has a right to a total of 5,000 shares for a total profit of $25,000. This clearly demonstrates the capacity and power of options as well as how profitable this kind of trade can be.

Great Risk vs. Reward Consideration

Like all good traders, it is essential to weight the risk posed by a certain trade compared to the possible rewards. When trading using options, then the style adapted will indicate the type of risk inherent in the trade. The above example clearly shows how profitable the options trading process is. If a loss was to be incurred in the above instance, then the total loss would have been the cost of the options.

In this instance, the risk is well worth the reward because the amount set to be lost is insignificant compared to the amount of profit to be made. In general, the higher the risk than the higher the potential return. Any time that a trader considers a trade, then the risk versus reward ratio should be taken into consideration.

As an options trader, you should learn how to benefit from volatility. Volatility needs to be your friend and partner as you can benefit from sharp and sudden movements in the markets. Options are mostly affected by implied volatility, which is essentially the most crucial factor affecting options prices. You need to learn to be on the lookout for implied volatility and determine whether it is low or high. This way, you will easily be able to get a sense of direction regarding the type of options to engage with.

Versatility and Flexibility

Another extremely appealing benefit of trading in options is the inherent flexibility. Options offer lots of flexibility with dozens of different strategies to pursue. This compares really well with numerous other trade and investment options out there. Most of these do not offer as much flexibility as options do. Also, most other securities have limited strategies, and this tends to limit the flexibility that a trader has on that security.

Take stocks, for instance. Even stock traders encounter certain limitations that are not inherent in options trading. There are plenty of strategies ranging from simple to compound to complex strategies. Stock traders generally buy, hold, or sell stocks. There isn't much else that they can do. This contrasts greatly with options because of the tens of strategies available to them. The versatility and flexibility inherent in options trading far surpass that of most other securities.

Firstly, options' flexibility allows them to be traded based on a wide variety of underlying securities. The variety and range of options strategies are massive. Also, the spreads provide real flexibility in the manner in which they can be traded. Traders have flexibility and versatility when it comes to limiting risks of assuming market positions when it comes to hedging, and even simply trying to benefit from stock movements, there are numerous opportunities available.

Chapter 1

Learn the Basics

What Are Stocks

Sometimes, the stock is referred to as shares or equity or. That is a sort of defense indicating proportionate control as it affects the company that issues it. When an individual has stocks, he / she have the right to a portion of the company's profits and properties. One can purchase shares and trade them at stock markets, but it doesn't really mean there are no other places to sell and buy stocks. In private sales too, stocks may be exchanged. In the business sector, there is barely any investor that does not have shares in one's portfolio. They will be in accordance with regulatory rules that have been placed in motion to protect consumers against corrupt procedures until transactions can be considered to be legal. Markets have surpassed them when contrasted with other financial products.

Bond vs. Stock

Companies are giving out shares to raise the capital necessary to enhance their firm or to engage in new initiatives. Stocks can be obtained in various ways, occasionally, when a personal problem in the main market, a person can buy it straight from the firm. In other cases, the investment company may buy it from other stockholders on the second-hand market. Know that it plays it out if you have a corporation selling stock, as it needs to collect capital. Bonds are on a separate planet of their own. Bondholders are considered by the corporation as investors, who prefer to get interested rather than dividends. The principal is charged for them, too. When it tends to come to a company's owners, investors have greater control of the properties and profits as fraud happens than stakeholders. The company would first compensate creditors before charging owners throughout a recession. Shareholders wind up becoming the last one in line and can finally get none or a limited sum. That suggests stocks are at greater costs than debt. You must stop going for stocks if you can't tolerate this.

What Are Options

Options are all those agreements that require the bearer to be interested at a fixed price in buying or selling a lump sum of the asset. The holder has the right to purchase or not, as far as the deal is not finished. Options are traded as other asset groups, utilizing investment portfolio brokers. Options are good insofar as they can boost an individual's portfolio. By leveraging and adding income protection, they can get this done. Specific option circumstances can match an investor's objectives, depending on the situations at hand. Let's say that a share market is decreasing; options could be used as a viable hedge to rein in downside loss. One may use options to obtain recurring revenue. They can also be used for speculative motives, such as wagering in which the stock price would be going. The way free lunch in bonds and stocks doesn't exist in the same way; there aren't any free lunches with options. There are certain risks one might face when it comes to trading options. Before you hop into trading options, you must understand those risks. This is one reason you're shown a disclaimer when you've wanted to do trading options with a brokerage company that's similar to all of this: options are participants of a larger securities league, called derivatives. A derivative's price is related to the cost of another item. Let's explain some further. A tomato type is ketchup. The grape equivalent is wine. A commodity derivative is an option on cash. Options can be considered financial equity contracts, implying their interest relies on the price of some currency. Some instances of derivative products are calls, puts, advances, futures, etc.

Options vs. Forex

An investor might assume the U.S. dollar would get stronger as a comparison to the Euro, so the individual earns if the outcomes turn out. If the study pans out, the plan, if it succeeds, will continue to change trade. Once you get interested in trading options, you continue to get engaged in purchasing and selling options on vast numbers of futures, securities, and so on, which can then go up or down at a price over the process. It is equivalent to trading forex since you might easily influence the purchasing power to get a governing power over the economic future or stocks. There is a range of variations in selling Options and investing with Forex. These are

- 24 / 7 Trading

When you indulge in Forex rather than dealing with Futures, you get the opportunity to transact any moment of a day, 5 days a week. Looking just at the Forex sector, you'll know it's going longer than on any stock system on the planet. If you've opted to make double-digit returns on the sector, it's crucial to have a fair period of time per week to make certain trades. When a major incident takes place somewhere within the globe, you may wind up becoming among the first to profit from the foreign currency exchange situation. You don't have to waste time waiting and expecting the demand will open up in the sector, as in the case with stocks for trading. You can deal comfortably with Forex if you so choose, at all periods of day and night. You can exchange it any time you want.

- Fast Trade Completion

When you take advantage of the Forex trade market immediately, you appear to get immediate trade actions. As in the scenario of Options and any other markets, you do not have to be postponed. When you put the request, it wound up being loaded with the cheapest available quality on the market, rather than asking what company would end up buying. You won't need to experience the temptation to hesitate in the options scenario. Once you are engaged in overseas trading platforms, unlike in the case of trading options, there's also a good opportunity for liquidity.

- Non-Commission

Forex business is one who doesn't require fee because it operates like an interbank system, where purchasers are immediately paired against sellers. There are no instances in capital exchange and other sectors with trading commissions. You're going to see a gap between asking price and offer, that's how many Forex brokerages make their profits.

What Is a Broker

One of the most important decisions you are going to make when you first get started with day trading is picking out a broker. This will determine the types of securities you can trade (for example, many brokers aren't going to work with cryptocurrencies for trading), how much you pay for each of your trades, and what kind of platform you get to use. Picking out a reputable broker, someone who is easy to work with can make a big difference in the results you can get with your trades.

The biggest thing to consider when you work with a broker, after determining that they do trade in the securities you are interested in, is their compensation plan. You want to check this out to see if it is going to be beneficial to you and your trading method. Since day trading requires a lot of small transactions during the day, you don't want to end with a compensation plan where the broker gets a set fee every time you execute a trade.

There are a lot of different fee structures that your broker can choose, and you need to learn and agree to the one that makes the most sense to you. Going with a set fee for the whole year would be ideal, but you can also work it out that you pay a percentage of your earnings, so if you don't earn anything on a trade, you won't be missing out. No matter which broker you decide to go with though, make sure to discuss the fee structure with them from the very beginning.

One of the requirements you are using for selecting a broker's company must include:

- Margin and Account Necessities

The criteria for the accounts and the margin can differ between brokerage to brokerage. Many investment companies may need initial minimum investments of $2,000, and others will need minimums of $10,000.

Margin criteria for stock options transactions can differ from one trading company to another. The criteria for the investment margin can often differ based on the sort of options approach that you are utilizing. For starters, certain broker companies would require you to sign a document indicating your trading expertise level in options. When you have completed the program, grasped extensively the tactics that you plan to use, and have effectively traded paper, you will comfortably say that you are a competent trader of options. You can sell and buy shorter and longer calls/puts while provided margin rights. The arrangement that you sign is insurance for the trading company to ensure that margin protected entities grasp all the consequences of the transactions they position. For example, in bullish economic conditions, a newbie trader who sells naked calls might quickly hit a snag. If you knew this course, you would be much less likely to position these trades because the potential risks are limitless. It does among the advantages of sharing trading you will still be conscious of the overall costs and potential earnings.

In case you don't have the money required to meet your chosen brokerage company's criteria for maximum margin rights, you will still be able to buy long calls and puts. Brokerage companies would usually need more money or better trading expertise opportunities for short selling calls and puts. When you are in this scenario, just using the long calls and puts into constructing your fund before you can set up a maximum margin protected stock options account or find another brokerage company.

When buying longer puts or longer calls, brokerage firms may ask you to pay for the premium option in relation to the brokerage costs as a start. Before conducting trade-in options, several brokerage companies would need greater minimal equity throughout the account. So, whenever you need to purchase 1 XYZ Jan 20 calls at $1.50 per equity, you'd require $150 + remuneration costs to get into the business.

When placing short or selling, you would usually be forced to retain 50 percent of the intrinsic value of the portfolio – the percentage for which choice is now out of the obtained cash + premium. For e.g., if XYZ stock trades at $20 a share and you decide to cut a $1 a share loan on November 15, the margin criteria will be:

[(50% x $20) — ($20-$ 15) + $1] / 100 = $600

You will preserve the disparity between prices of strikes less the credit earned for payment spreads. For instances, if you placed a bull on ABC stock selling a placed-on March 20 and buying a put-on March 15 for a $1 credit each share their profit margin per agreement will be:

[($20-$ 15)-$ 1] x 100, = $400

In addition, earnings are measured once the competition is closed. If you've got a stance that has shifted strongly toward you, a "call margin" may be issued by the brokerage necessitating you to transfer extra capital for your position. If you are incapable or unable to do so, a portion of your acct will be expropriated to fulfill the standards of the call.

Chapter 2

Build Your Own Business

How to Start

Walking you through the learning curve of options trading will always start with the most basic move you'll need to make setting yourself up in a position to actually be able to trade. To do that, you're going to need an options account.

One thing to know before you pick your firm: times have changed considerably over the last couple of decades when it comes to options trading. Back before the internet became such a constant part of our lives, your brokerage firm – or, at least, your personal representative at the firm – would make your options trades on your behalf and you paid a hefty price for their services. Nowadays, however, you'll be doing most of your trades yourself.

Commission for your representative is thus a whole lot lower than it used to be, which means it won't cost you an arm and both legs to rely on your rep in the early days of your experience. While you are learning, feel free to make use of your firm's services to place and confirm your trades, if it helps you feel more comfortable getting to know the process.

With this in mind, there are going to be certain things to look for when you select your firm:

- Compare commission prices to make sure you're getting a great deal.
- Make sure the firm has up to date software and is capable of setting

up trades quickly and reliably to make sure you get those trades you want at the best prices.

- Check out the hours of service to ensure they are compatible with your needs. In these days of online firms, you could be dealing with a firm that's across the ocean from the markets you have an interest in, or you might find that a firm only makes its reps available for the length of the working day, which might not suit your own timing.

- Speak personally with the reps at the firm, as these are the people who are going to help you during the process of setting up your strategy. You want someone who is personable and knowledgeable – and, most importantly, who speaks in terms that you personally find easy to comprehend.

- Take a look at the additional services the firm supplies. Many will offer learning materials, guides and even classes or webinars to help you hone your strategies. Even if you feel that you know all you need to know already, there's no harm in a refresher course or a little nugget of inspiration every once in a while.

Once you select a firm, you'll then need to consider signing a "margin agreement" with that firm. This agreement allows you to borrow money from the firm in order to purchase your stocks, which is known as "buying on margin".

Understandably, your brokerage firm is not going to allow you to do that if you don't have the financial status to pay them back. They will therefore run a credit check on you and ask you for information about your resources and knowledge.

A margin account is not a necessity for options trading – you don't actually use margin to purchase an option, because it must be paid for in full.

However, it can be useful as you graduate to more advanced strategies – in some cases, it will be obligatory. If you opt to sign a margin agreement, talk it through thoroughly with the firm as there are certain restrictions on the type of money you can use that may apply to you.

Next, you'll need to sign an "options agreement" – and, this time, it's an obligatory step. This agreement is designed to figure out how much you know about options and how much experience you have of trading them. It also aims to ensure that you are absolutely aware of the risks you take by trading and make sure that you are financially able to handle those risks.

By ascertaining these things, your firm can determine what level of options trading you should be aiming for. It will therefore approve your "trading level", of which there are five:

- Level 1: You may sell covered calls
- Level 2: You may buy calls and puts and also buy strangles, straddles and collars. You may also sell puts that are covered by cash and by options on exchange-traded funds and indexes
- Level 3: You may utilize credit and debit spreads
- Level 4: You may sell "naked puts", straddles and strangles
- Level 5: You may sell "naked indexes" and "index spreads"

Don't worry if you're not sure yet what each of these things means – you will be by the time you finish reading this book. For now, all you need to be aware of is that your firm will determine for you which level you should be at. As a beginner, don't be surprised if you only reach the first two levels.

Once you've signed the agreement, you'll be handed a booklet that contains a mine of information about risks and rewards within options trading. Right now, if you were to read that booklet, it would seem to be in a foreign language. By the time you finish this crash course, it will be a lot more decipherable – and it's very important for your success that you do read it.

Finally, your firm will present you with a "standardized option contract". It's the same for every trader, which means you stand the same chance of success as every other person out there in the options market.

By trading an option, you are entering into a legal agreement that is insured by the Options Clearing Corporation, which guarantees the contract will be honored in full. Make sure you read that contract to be aware of not only the rights you have as a trader, but also the obligations you must follow in the same role.

Congratulations, you have an options account. This is the conduit through which you will create and implement your strategies and begin your adventure in options trading.

Options vs. Stocks

Stocks

A stock is, at its most basic level, ownership in a company. When an investor buys a stock of a company, he is technically a part owner in that company. So if an investor buys Facebook's stock, he owns a small portion of Facebook. The proportion of an investor's ownership grows with the number of shares he owns. For example, if a company issued 1,000 shares of stock and, if an investor owned 100 shares, or 10% of the shares, it means that he owns 10% of the company. If an investor owns 200 of the 1,000 shares, or 20% of the shares, he owns 20% of the company. However, this does not mean that he is entitled to 20% of the company's profits; an investor cannot go to Facebook's headquarters if he owns their stock and demand for some money. Rather, owning a portion of a company entitles an investor to a portion of the company's dividends. A dividend is a payment that a company's board of directors will make if they want to distribute a portion of the company's profits to shareholders. Whenever a company decides to pay a dividend, shareholders are entitled to that money based on the amount of shares they own. The dividends are paid in proportion to the number of shares an investor owns. If you own 25% of a company that pays a dividend of one hundred dollars, you are entitled to $25.

A dividend differs from a profit because dividends are a portion of the profit that a company decides to pay out to shareholders; a firm can decide to distribute a part of its profits to shareholders. Profit is the revenue (money) a company makes minus its costs (expenses). Usually, profits are reinvested back into the company, used to pay off debts, or distributed to shareholders as dividends. Moreover, a dividend is a profit for the investor, which is distributed from the firm's profits, while a regular profit is for the company;

profits are reinvested in the company and a dividend is reinvested in an investor's portfolio.

It is important to recognize that not all companies pay a dividend; if and how much the company pays is determined by what the firm's management desires. They can pay $5 for each share, or one cent. In fact, many companies will decide not to pay a dividend.

Options

Options are contracts that will allow you to purchase or sell a stock at a fixed price on a previously decided date. Options are very flexible. The contract between the investor and seller does not obligate either to buy or sell the stock, respectively. As the name suggests, this is only an option. Most contracts drawn up as options are for a fixed limit, mostly 100 shares. When you purchase an option, you are only purchasing the contract and not the stock. You can then either buy that stock or sell it on the fixed date at the price that is agreed upon. You can also let the option expire.

An option is quite complex, but at a very basic level, you will lock the price of the stock whose price you think will increase in value. If you made the right call, you would profit from purchasing the stock at a rate lower than the actual rate. If you make the wrong call, you can let go of the option since you will only lose the cost of the contract.

How Option's Price Determined

There are many factors that determine the options price. Of them all, the implied volatility (IV) is most important. A good way to make a judgment on the volatility of an option is to first check its IV and compare it with its volatility history. A final step will be to also compare it with the volatility on the broad market. These should provide you with important information that will help to choose a suitable options and trading strategy.

Premium will be pushed up with high implied volatility. If the trader believes that the volatility will not increase further, this situation makes writing an option very attractive. As you can imagine, if the implied volatility is low, the premiums are low too. This presents a good buying opportunity especially when the trader expects the underlying to move up enough to rake in some profit.

- Identify events

The stock specific events include announcements on earnings, national speeches, and major company actions such as mergers, expansions or layoffs.

The announcement of an impending event alone can have a significant effect on implied volatility. This is because of various speculations of the impact of that even on the stock market. When the even finally occurs, it can have such a huge impact on the stock prices as to alter trends and cause spikes. This surge of activities presents unique high-risk opportunities to traders. Depending on your risk tolerance, you can decide to ride the short-term wave to observe the long-term trend. Because events can disrupt market trends, it is important to know those events that impact your choice options so as to know when to exit your position.

Chapter 3

Binary Options

Binary options are similar to traditional options in many ways except that they ultimately boil down to a basic yes or no question. Instead of worrying about what exact price an underlying stock is going to have, a binary option only cares if it is going to be above one price at the time of its expiration. Traders then make their trades based on if they believe the answer is yes or no, at which time it will be worth either $0 or $100. While it may seem simple on its face, it is important that you fully understand how binary options work, as well as the time frames and markets they work with. It is also important to understand the specific advantages and disadvantages that they have and which companies are legally allowed to offer binary options for trade.

They are also a great way for those who are interested in day-trading but don't have the serious capital required to get off the ground, to ply their trade. Traditional stock day trading limits don't apply with binary options, so you are allowed to start trading with just 1, $100 deposit. It is also important to keep in mind that binary options are a derivative created by its association with an underlying asset, which means they don't give you ownership of that asset in any way. As such, you would be unable to exercise them as a means of generating dividends or utilizing voting rights.

The Benefits of Picking Binary Options

The potential for a high return: this is a risky form of investing, but if you learn to read the market properly, you will find that it has a lot of potential for a lot of money to come to you. If you do well with this trading option, you could see a return on investment between 60 to 90 percent.

The risk is fixed: You will know right at the beginning how much money you stand to lose or to win depending on which way the prediction goes. This helps make it easier to decide on your choices. Other investments can end up being a lot of guesswork, and if things go south, you can lose a lot more than you put into the whole thing. On the other hand, with binary options, you know exactly how much you stand to gain and lose right off the top.

You can even win after losing: Since you will find that the risks on these options are high, some brokers offer a return on money that you invested if your predictions were wrong. This is not going to be the full amount, but getting a small percentage of your money back can be encouraging compared to losing it all.

Easy trading: These are easier to trade on. Other options in the stock market make this hard, but the platforms for binary options help the investor trade without all the hassle. You can work with a live chat feature to do this or even with your broker if you have some questions. Besides, there are really only two options for most of your trading options, so this makes things easier as well.

Rewards: The risk associated with any binary option is always going to cap out at the cost of the initial trade because the worst result for any option is for it to time out and be worth $0. The reward is also capped and based on the amount of the initial investment. As an example, if you purchase a $20 binary option, then you are always going to make $100 at most, which means you will make $80 and have a 4:1 risk/reward ratio, which is better than you will find in most other situations most of the time.

This will only be in your benefit for a limited time, however, as gains will never increase pass $100 regardless of how much movement an underlying asset may have. The easiest way to mitigate this particular downside is to simply double down on options contracts from the start.

How to Trade Binary Options

Binary options are currently traded on the Nadex exchange, which was the first exchange created expressly to sell binary options in the United States. It offers market access as well as its own trading platform, which always has access to the most recent binary options pricing.

It is also possible to trade options on the Chicago Board Options Exchange, which can be accessed by those with an options trading approved brokerage account through more traditional means. When doing so, it is important to keep in mind that not all brokers are going to offer options trading, which means that if this is a route you are considering going down, you will need to plan accordingly and choose your broker with these services in mind.

Trading via Nadex costs 90 cents per trade with a maximum fee of $9 per transaction, this means that lots greater than 10 are essentially free. The fee is not deducted from the trading account until the trade has expired, and if the trade does not end profitably, then there is no charge as well. Trading on the Chicago Board is subject to traditional brokerage fees.

Choosing the right market: Nothing is stopping you from trading across various asset classes at once when it comes to binary options and, indeed, Nadex allows trading across most of the major indices including the S&P 500, Nasdaq 100, Russell 2000 and the Dow 30. Available global indices include those from the UK, Germany, and Japan. Trades are also available for a variety of forex pairs, including AUD/JPY, EUR/GBP, USD/CHF, GBP/JPY, USD/CAD, AUD/USD, EUR/JPY, USD/JPY, GBP/UDS, and EUR/USD.

Another popular option through Nadex is the commodity binary options, which include crude oil, natural gas, and gold, copper, silver, corn, and soybeans. There are also several options when it comes to trading based on a specific news event which means you can buy options on things like if the:

Binary Option Timeframes

Weekly Trading

Weekly binary options are listings that provide the opportunity for trading in the short-term along with lots of opportunities to hedge the choices you do make. As you might infer from the name, weekly trading means working with options that expire in exactly one week, with the standard being for them to be listed on Thursday and expire the next Friday. While this type of binary options trading has been around for quite some time, they were largely only used by investors who followed the cash indices. This exclusivity has changed in the past decade as the Chicago Board has started expanding the practice of this type of trading until now there are nearly 1,000 opportunities to do so each week.

Beyond just having a specific timeframe, weekly binary options are different than more traditional options in that they can only be purchased 21 days out of the month, which is why they aren't listed as expiring in the monthly style. As such, in the week that monthly options are set to expire, they are technically classified as weekly options.

The biggest benefit of this type of binary option is that it makes it extremely easier to purchase exactly what you are looking for in a specific trade without needing to come up with additional capital just to end up with more than you actually need. For those who are interested in selling, weekly binary options make it easier to do so more regularly as opposed to having to wait a month or more between sales.

Weekly binary options trades are also worth considering in that they ultimately lead to lower costs for trades with larger spreads like calendar or diagonal spreads as you can sell weekly binary options against them in the interim. They also come in handy when it comes to higher volumes of trades overall, especially when it comes to hedging larger positions in risky markets. Likewise, if the market is range-bound, the weekly market will still be fruitful thanks to strategies like the iron condor or iron butterfly.

The biggest downside to weekly binary options is that you won't have much of a chance of things changing in your favor if you choose poorly from the start. Likewise, if you are looking to short the binary option in question, then it is important to keep in mind that it would only take a relatively small overall move to push something into the money.

As you will have less time with which to turn a profit when dealing with weekly binary options when you do make a move it is vital that your timing is as precise as possible as if you choose poorly then you can easily find yourself paying for something that will end up being worthless practically as soon as you put your money down. It is also important to consider how much risk the option offers, as buying in bulk is always cheaper if you have the data to back it up.

Along similar lines, it is important to avoid naked puts or calls when trading in the weekly timeframe as these often end up with a lower probability of success overall. If you are quite specific when it comes to the directions of your chosen trades, then a structured trade or a debit spread may be a better choice.

Selling weekly at a reliable pace for the long-term can lead to reliable profits when done correctly. It is likely to only work out if you strive to define your profits from the start, which means you always need to know the odds on all of your current options to avoid selling yourself short by mistake. Selling weekly makes it easier to secure reliable profits while requiring extra margin to prevent unmitigated losses if you end up choosing poorly.

The most reliable type of trades to move forward within this scenario it is important to look into trades with lots of implied volatility as it is more likely to work out in your favor in the long run due to the either/or nature of binary options. Spreads are another useful way to make money from the weekly market as the overall implied volatility will typically be higher when compared to the monthly variation, which means the spread can help deal with an unexpected change in direction with speed required to do something about it. Selling against a long option, meanwhile, will serve to decrease the amount of volatility in the transaction, which means the ideal point to use the debit spread will be near the current price, assuming the ratio of risk to reward is close to 1 to 1.

Chapter 4

Trader's Mindset

Strategies to Think Like an Option Trader

Let me educate you regarding somewhat a mystery, which isn't that a very remarkable mystery all things considered. In the event that you genuinely need to turn into a fruitful broker, you ought not exclusively to be exceeding expectations at making sense of the best systems, yet you ought to likewise be having a triumphant outlook. A broad examination can assist you with getting your realities straight however when you are exchanging, your outlook can assume a tremendous job. Truth be told, it isn't the exchanging methodologies or immaculate market examination or straightforward intelligence that causes you to win exchanges, however, it is your mental attitude that will get you far.

The vast majority of the tenderfoots to whom I have collaborated with have consistently disclosed to me something very similar – they are attempting to make sense of the correct procedure, and they, for the most part, remain very worried about doing as such. Most amateurs imagine that once you have the best technique, you should simply apply it and cash will come racing into your financial balance. However, that is not what occurs.

When you are in the exchanging scene for a long while, you will comprehend that exchanging isn't about methodologies and numbers, and some of the time, it can even be intense. There are such a large number of merchants simply like you who are sitting tight for their brilliant chance to turn into a mogul, and they are for the most part smart and very much learned. They even have planned full-confirmation methodologies which are question strong. Be that as it may, you will see that even they wind up losing cash every once in a while.

Manage the Risk

You will most likely hear everybody state this again and again that legitimate hazard the board is the thing that you need so as to be effective. Furthermore, brokers won't have the option to utilize the hazard the board techniques on the off chance that they are not precise with chance appraisal in any case. Remembering the factor of instability, you need to comprehend what an express or verifiable position is. You likewise need to evaluate what the significant drawback of exchange can be. These are just a couple of inquiries that you ought to present yourself.

When the hazard is made sense, you need to ready to discover a route so as to moderate the hazard or control it. For instance, on the off chance that you are more into transient exchanges the universe of alternatives, there will be a lot of misfortune making exchanges that you will go over in a day. Allow us to state, you chose to hold your position for the time being, and on that equivalent night, some unfriendly news was discharged, which totally altered the course of the market, thus your wager turns sour. In any case, your hazard the board system ought to be acceptable to the point that it can control the hazard regardless of what the circumstance is. Enhancement is only one of the procedures that dealers use to limit the dangers engaged with an exchange, thus their exchange size is diminished.

Another attribute that you ought to have so as to be a fruitful choices broker is that you ought to be acceptable at overseeing cash. Regardless of how much capital you have, on the off chance that you don't oversee it admirably, it is, at last, going to go down the channel. One of the extremely normal models that I can give you is – assume a dealer utilized 90% of his capital on a solitary exchange and the exchange reverse discharges, so he will wind up losing practically the entirety of his cash.

Keep an Eye of Your Trades

The effective merchants have the propensity for recording their exchanges in a diary or anyplace. Do you know why? So that at whatever point a comparative circumstance emerges, you recall what you did, and perhaps you can apply the system once more. Every one of your exchanges that have been finished has an abundance of data in particular in the event that you can remember it and use it in your exchanges. This will place all the chances in support of you.

Keep on Learning

It has been said by the CBOT or the Chicago Board of Trade that out of each and every individual who is exchanging, 90% of them are going to observe misfortunes. However, the significant thing here is to gain from the misfortunes and mix-ups that you have made as opposed to remaining trying to claim ignorance about it. Practice and more practice is what is going to assist you with advancing beyond others, and for that, you have to comprehend why those misfortunes occurred so you can amend your exchange from the following exchange onwards. The market is rarely stale and continually continues advancing. You need to develop with it as well, by being a functioning student.

Have Discipline

Having a legitimate order will get you far in your alternatives exchanging vocation. Be that as it may, what does being trained means? It implies that you have played out an adequate measure of research, effectively distinguished the open doors in the market that can work in support of yourself, set up the exchange the correct way, structure objectives, utilize the correct methodology, and furthermore have a leave system. Do you know when you don't have discipline? It is the points at which you don't work on anything of your own however just follow the crowd. Regardless of whether somebody gives you a tip, try not to be confiding in it until and except if you haven't played out your own examination. At the point when you acquire a misfortune, it's on you and not on the individual who gave you a tip in such a case that you had played out your examination; you would have distinguished what wasn't right with the tip. That is the reason having a free system is so significant for everybody.

There are a few merchants who have finished training in this field, yet there are likewise such a large number of effective brokers who didn't read for alternatives exchanging are as yet becoming famous. In this way, it is absolutely your call whether you need to seek after your degree or not, however paying little heed to that, having an exhaustive thought regarding how the market functions are significant for everybody. On the off chance that you basically do a Google search 'on the most proficient method to bring in enormous cash in choices exchanging' and imagine that you have gotten the hang of everything, at that point you are incorrect. You need to delve into the subtleties and pick up everything that is there to think about the market and its activities.

Ability to Control Emotions

Controlling your feelings is a significant piece of exchanging brain research. Controlling your feelings doesn't possibly apply to times when everything is awful; however, it likewise applies to the great occasions whenever you may have higher odds of committing errors since you are so amped up for your success. On the off chance that you solicit most from the amateurs in the market, they will all reveal to you something very similar; they had made more misfortunes when they were energized and upbeat in view of success. Regardless of what number of series of wins you have, you need to remain grounded and not become presumptuous.

On the off chance that any of your exchanges end up being incorrect, you need to concede the issue and afterward pull out. Never let yourself get excessively connected to a specific stock; else, it will demolish you. Adhere to the standards you made first and foremost and don't redirect from your way since you are passionate.

Check the Volatility

At the point when you are attempting to see if you should purchase alternatives or sell them, unpredictability assumes a major job, and you are going to perceive how. Unpredictability is one such factor that can profit both put and call alternatives. On the upside, the alternative turns out to be considerably more significant, and on the drawback, there is a restricted hazard. In more straightforward terms, if instability builds, the estimation of alternative increments excessively independent of the way that the cost of the stock is at a similar point. In this way, when such an occasion happens, you need to purchase choices and, actually, sell the alternatives when you notice abatement in unpredictability.

Occurrence of Major Events

It is constantly exhorted that before any significant occasions happen or before any geopolitical issue emerges, you ought not to sell your choices and rather get them. Simply envision what might have occurred if, before the Greek emergency, you had sold your put alternatives. In the event that you purchase the alternatives as opposed to selling, at that point all you will lose is the premium paid. Be that as it may, on the off chance that you decide to sell them, at that point, there is a danger of your whole capital being cleared out.

Are You Taking A Defensive View Or An Affirmative One?

Your choice to sell or purchase a choice will be significantly affected by your view on the record or stock. Let me clarify the importance of the two perspectives with the goal that we are clear. At the point when you believe that a specific stock is going to conclusively go down or definitively go up, that is the point at which you have an agreed view. On the off chance that your view is certifiable, contingent on the case, you can either purchase a put choice or a call alternative. Be that as it may, then again, on the off chance that you have a protective view, at that point you ought to sell the choice. For instance, on the off chance that you imagine that a specific stock A won't ascend above $10, at that point it would be a superior choice on the off chance that you sell your $12 call alternative on this stock as opposed to purchasing.

Expiration Date

The termination date or the time left to expiry is a significant factor of alternatives that assumes a job in nearly everything. In any case, this factor of time works in the kindness of venders and against purchasers. The time rot is very steady at the outset, however as the time among now and the expiry date begins diminishing, the rot happens quicker. In easier terms, the estimation of the alternative declines quicker. Things being what they are, when alternatives are near their lapse date, it's anything but a smart thought to get them, right?

It is a vital choice with regards to whether you need to purchase choices or sell them, yet whichever choice you make, you need to thoroughly consider it.

Chapter 5

Options "Put" And Options "Call"

Put and call options are referred to as a derivative investment. The movements of their prices depend on the movements of prices of a different financial product, also referred to as the underlying.

So, what is an option? It is defined as the right to sell or buy a certain stock with a set price given a specific time frame. With options, you won't have outright ownership of the shares, but you make calculated bets on a stock's price and what its value will be in the future, given the specified expiration of the option. What makes options attractive is that you are to choose whether you want to exercise them or not. If your bet is wrong, you can let the options expire. Although the options' original cost is lost, it still wouldn't compare had you paid for the stock's full price.

Call options are purchased when the trader is expecting the underlying's price to go up within a particular time frame.

Put options are purchased when the trader is expecting the underlying's price to go down within a particular time frame.

There's an option for puts and calls to be written or sold. This will still generate income, but certain rights have to be given up to the option's buyer.

For options defined for the US, a call is defined as an options contract giving the buyer rights to buy an underlying asset at a previously set price any time until the expiration date. For options defined for the EU, buyers can choose to exercise the option to purchase the underlying but only on the set expiration date.

The strike price is defined as a price previously determined at which the call buyer has the choice to purchase the underlying asset. For example, a buyer of a certain stock calls option with a 10$ strike price may opt to purchase that stock at the same price before the expiration date of the option.

The expiration of options may vary. It can also be short or long term. It can be worth the while for call buyers to exercise the option, which is to require the writer or seller of the call to sell the stocks at the set strike price. But only if the underlying's current price is more than the strike price. For example, if a stock trades at $10 at the stock market, it is not profitable for the buyer of the call option to exercise the choice to purchase that stock at $11 since they could get the same on the market at a lower price.

Put buyers reserve the right to sell stocks at strike price during a set time range.

The highs and lows the stock market goes through can be both exciting and nerve-wracking for newbie or veteran investors. Risking hard-earned money can make anyone anxious. But played right with sound and well-planned strategies, you can be successful in this field

If you are looking for a way to invest in the stock market but you are trying to avoid the risk of directly selling stocks or buying them, options trading might be perfect for you. Options are typically traded at significantly lower prices compared to the underlying prices of the actual shares. This makes trading them a less risky way to control a large stock position, although you don't own the shares. Using options strategically allows risk mitigation while maintaining huge profit potentials and you will be playing in the field even if you're investing just a fraction of the stock's price.

All of these benefits of options trading got you excited, right? After all, options have a lower risk and they're a lot cheaper. There are two major disadvantages, however – the limited-time aspect and the reality that you don't own the stock until you choose to exercise your options.

Call Options

With call options, what you pay for is just 'rights to buy' certain shares at a set price and covered by a specific time frame. Let's say that stock ABC is selling for $90 per share in May. If you believe that the stock's price will go up over a few months, you will purchase a three-month option to buy 100 shares of ABC by August 31 for $100. For this sample call option, you would be paying around $200 if the option cost per share is $2. In options, you are only allowed to buy in increments of 100 shares. This gives you the choice to purchase 100 shares of ABC anytime within the three-month timeframe. The $200 investment is significantly lower than the $9,000 you would have had to shell out if you bought 1000 shares outright.

If you bet right and on July 15, if the ABC shares hit the market at $115, you may exercise the call option and you would have gained $1,300 (that's 100 shares multiplied by the $15 profit you gained per share and deducted by your original investment of $200). If you don't have the resources to buy the shares, you can also make a profit if you re-sell the option to another investor or via the open market. The gain will be pretty much similar to this option.

If you bet wrong, and the price of ABC's shares fell to $80 never to reach $100 within the three-month timeframe, you can let the option reach its expiration, which saves you money (if you bought the shares outright, your original investment of $9,000 is now down to a value of only $8,000, so you lost $1000). This means you only lost $200, which was your investment for the call option.

Risks Involved in Call Options

Like any other form of investment, options have their share of potential risks. Taking the second scenario where you bet wrong as an example and stock

ABC never got to $100 during the option's timeframe of three months, you would have lost the entire $200 of your investment, right? In terms of loss percentage, that's %100. Anyone who's been playing the stock market would tell you that it's extremely rare for an investor to suffer a 100% loss. This scenario can only happen if ABC suddenly went bankrupt, causing the price of their stocks to plummet down to zero value.

Therefore, if you look at it from the point of view of percentages, options can cause you huge losses. Let's elaborate on this point. If the price of ABC's share went up to $99 and it's the last day for you to exercise the option, choosing to purchase the shares will mean losing a dollar for each share. What if you invested $9,000 for the stock and you owned 100 stock shares? In three months, which is the option's expiration date if you took it, you would have gained 10% from your original investment ($99 from $90). Comparing both, you would have gained 10% if you purchased the shares outright and lost %100 if you chose the option but did not exercise it. This example shows how risky options can be.

However, the opposite can happen if stock ABC reached a price higher than $100. If you purchased the option, your gain percentage would have been substantially higher compared to buying the stocks outright. If the stock reached $110, you would have gained 400% ($10 gain versus the $2 per share investment) if you went for the option and only gained 22% ($20 gain versus the $90 per share investment) if you purchased the shares.

Lastly, when you own the stock, nothing can force you to sell. That means if after three months, and stock ABC's price goes down, you can hang on to it if you believe it still has the potential to recover and even increase in value compared to the original. If the price goes up dramatically, you'll make significant gains and you didn't incur losses. However, if you chose options as your investment method, the expiration would have forced you to suffer a 100% loss after the set timeframe. There will be no option to hold on to the stock even if you believe it will go up in value soon.

Options have major pros and also major cons. You need to be aware of these before you step into the arena of options trading.

Put Options

On the other side of the options investment is the put option. Whereas call is the right to purchase, 'put' gives you the option to sell a certain security at a set price within a specific time frame. Investors usually purchase put options to protect the price of a stock in case it suddenly drops down, or even the market itself. With put options, you can sell the shares and your investment portfolio is protected from unexpected market swings. Put options are, therefore, a way to hedge your portfolio or lower its risk.

For example, you have invested in stock ABC for 100 shares, which you bought for $50 per share. As of May 31, the price per share has reached a market high $70. Of course, you'd want to maintain this position in your stock, and at the same time protect your gained profits in case the price of this stock goes down. To fit your requirements, you may purchase a put option with a three-month expiration and $70 per share strike price.

If ABC's stock price goes down drastically over the next couple of months, reaching a low per-share price of only $60, you will still be protected. By exercising your put option, you will still be able to sell the shares at $70 each even if stock ABC is now trading at a lower value. If you are feeling confident that ABC can still recover in the future, you can hold on to the stock and just resell the put option. The price of this put option will have gone up because of the diving stock ABC took.

On the other hand, if stock ABC's value kept climbing, just let the put option expire and you would still profit from the increased price of the shares. Even though you lost what you have invested in the put option, you still have the underlying stock with you. Therefore, you can view the put option as a kind of insurance policy for your investment, which may or may not use. Another thing to remember is that you can purchase put options even if you don't own the underlying stock, just like you would in a call option. You are not required to own the stock itself.

Risks Involved in Put Options

Just as with call options, put options carry the same risks. There is also a 100% loss potential when the underlying stock price goes up, and a huge gain when the price dives because you can resell the option for a higher price.

Chapter 6

The Most Effective Strategies

Covered Calls

The covered call is the perfect introductory trading strategy for beginners. It has a simple thesis that you can execute, and there's no need to adjust the trade in any way. While you don't need to adjust any options trading strategy listed in this book, the option is always available.

This adjustability often leads beginners to confuse themselves and complicate matters. None of this exists with the covered call. As a bonus, the covered call can be implemented simply as an extension of your regular investment activities in your retirement account.

Strategy

The underlying theory behind the covered call is the lowering of the cost basis of your stock purchase. For example, if you purchase 100 shares of AMZN for your retirement account or regular investing account, if you could lower the price you paid for the stock over time, you give yourself a lot more wiggle room with respect to how the market performs.

For example, if you purchased AMZN shares at $150 per share and the market declines to $145, you're carrying a $5 loss. Well, what if you could use a strategy that would make your purchase price effectively $140? In that case, you're still in a profit. The covered call is that strategy.

In fact, with a covered call, it is entirely possible to end up owning a stock for effectively zero cost.

Put Calendar Spread

In direct contrast to the call calendar spread trade, the put calendar spread trade seeks to take advantage of a decline in a stock's price. This is less widely used than the call calendar spread. Either way, it works in the same manner by creating a horizontal spread between the same strike prices but different expiration dates.

If you anticipate AMZN to decline to 1800 after a month, you can buy the put of the near or far month, which will cost you $40.40 per share. Since you reason that AMZN is not going to hit this mark within this month, you can buy the front-month put at the same level which is going to net you $21.95 per share.

This creates a net debit of $18.45 per share and is your maximum loss. Your maximum gain is subject to the same conditions as with the call calendar spread, that is to say, it is unlimited and depends on whether the price hits your shorter-term put before it expires. Either way, this horizontal spread is a great way to take advantage of bearish market movements.

Calendar Call Spread

The spreads we've seen thus far have been what are called vertical spreads. This implies how they show up on the option chain, where strike prices are listed on top of one another. By shorting one and buying another, you're earning the difference in the prices of the two and hence the term' spread'.

Vertical spreads require you to trade options within the same expiration month but horizontal spreads, which is what the calendar spread is, involves buying and selling options form different expiration months. The call calendar spread is a bullish strategy that can be used to great effect as we'll see.

Execution

The calendar call spread consists of two legs:

1. A current month or short term short call
2. A near month or longer-term long call

The idea is that while the stock takes its time to make it to the longer (time frame) call's strike price, you might as well collect the premium on the short call in the meantime. The instrument for profit is the longer call which captures the upward movement in the stock.

The longer term call can be from the near month or something from the longer cycle. The choice is yours. The only consideration here is the liquidity since you don't want to be trading in an instrument that has a huge spread thanks to low demand or trading volume. As long as the liquidity is fine and spreads are low or manageable, you should be fine.

As your first step to implementing the trade, you will purchase an at or in the money call in anticipation of the move upwards. The short call is at a level you think the price is not going to reach within that time frame. The idea is to earn the premium from the short call and the capital gain from the long call. If this trade works out, it is as close to a win-win as you can get in the markets. Let's see how the math works with AMZN.

Let's say our long call is from the near month. The price we'll pay for the 1830 call, which is the one nearest to market price and in the money, is $63.65. For our short call, let's say there a medium level resistance at 1840, which AMZN is going to have to work to get past and is unlikely to do this by the end of the month.

The premium we earn on this call is $36.30.

The cost of entry = Cost of long call - premium earned from short call = 63.65-36.3 = $27.35 per share.

Maximum loss = cost of entry

There are many scenarios for calculating the maximum gain as you can imagine since this depends on whether the short-term call ever moves into the money. Whatever the scenario, you will have to subtract your cost of entry from the final gain.

Horizontal spreads are thus different from vertical spreads thanks to their open-ended nature. It will take some getting used to, but with time, you'll find that they tend to be far more rewarding if you can get your analysis correct.

Straddles and Strangles

Now that you've got a good grasp on basic options trading strategies, it's time to look at the good stuff. Straddles and strangles are the most basic, intermediate trading strategies when it comes to options, and they are fascinating to execute. Almost every professional option trader loves them thanks to the high levels of neutrality and arbitrage they enable.

For those of you who are unfamiliar with the concept, arbitrage refers to taking advantage of price mismatches in the same product between two different markets. These days true arbitrage opportunities are rare but using options, you can implement this wonderful strategy to produce risk-free returns.

Let's look at a straddle first.

Long Straddles
The straddle is a true arbitrage strategy at heart. One of the key aspects of any arbitrage strategy is that the trader implementing it does not care which direction the price moves in. All they are concerned with is the degree of movement, the greater the degree of movement, the greater the profit.

This strategy is best used prior to times of high volatility. For example, if a company has a significant earnings announcement that is going to send its stock rocketing or cratering, but you don't know which way it is going to go, a straddle is the strategy for you.

Long Strangles
Much like a long straddle aims to take advantage of a burst of volatility in a stock, the long strangle has the same goal but aims to do it at a much lower cost. While the straddle requires you to buy options with the same strike price, the strangle spreads it out a bit and creates a band between the strike

prices of both legs.

Collars

We're taking the complexity up a notch with the collar. Collars involve a covered call, but there is an additional layer or leg to the trade which is a protective put. Collars are more attractive than covered calls because, under certain circumstances, they can be completely risk-free and truly market neutral.

Implementing this strategy does require you to have a decent grasp of market environments such as ranges and trends.

Strategy

The beauty of market-neutral strategies like the covered call and the collar is that they are conservative by nature and yet are powerful in terms of the returns they generate. You don't need to do anything fancy beyond learning a few technical-sounding names to impress others at cocktail parties!

A well-executed collar will pre-define your maximum gain and loss in advance. This way, you know exactly what will happen if the market behaves in a certain manner and can rest knowing that no matter what happens, your risk is defined fully and you need not worry about slippage or volatility.

Do note that there is the possibility of loss. The covered call does not have this component to it, but the collar does. Hence, the collar is the first strategy we'll deal with where defining your risk per trade becomes important. While I don't like putting a number of strategies, you can conservatively expect around 10-12% per year with the collar strategy.

This might sound like it's not worth it given that a basic index fund has returned the same over the years. Well, consider that this is a market-neutral strategy, so you're insulated against up and down movements, unlike in an index fund. Second, index fund data is averaged over eighty years. Within those stretches, there have been decades where real returns have been negative.

Chapter 7

Other Strategies

Iron Condor

Iron Condor's strategy is the primary strategy for options traders who want to take advantage of the stock market without having to choose a direction. Ideally, these options trading work best in non-trending markets. Still, it can also be used successfully during trends and more volatile markets if the trader has the knowledge and ability to spend the time he needs to correct them. Check and adjust!

This range takes advantage of theta decline in options - the fact that possibilities rot and lose value over time. When a flat iron condor is located and nearing its maturity - if the "sold" strike positions are far enough away from the "damaged road," these condors' can usually be worthless and leave the iron condor trader for a short time.

Iron capacitors are made up of two separate credit spreads - one at each end from which the underlying asset is currently traded. The trader call range was placed above the current base price. The spread of the bull is placed below the current trading price. Depending on which broker is used, they can be set individually as individual vertical spreads or together as a trade-in iron condor.

The purpose of the transaction is to keep the underlying asset within the "spread" created by the two credit spreads sold. While trading is on, the base point on the map can move as long as it remains in this "range." These are submarines that step too far in both directions; trade is at stake, and the trader will have to take some action to be able to steer and adapt.

This type of trading strategy offers a very high chance of success - and can usually be profitable. However, it is essential to realize that the risk of rewarding relationships between these deals is NOT ideal because losing a month, if not correctly managed, can wipe out profits throughout the year. It is crucial for the long-term success of this trading to learn how to set the right surplus targets, exit and stop points, and to gain the necessary knowledge on how to properly control and adjust the position of iron condors in difficulty.

When I first started trading in this strategy, I found that I had one month. Suddenly, I hit the wrong month and finally put everything back and then some - simply because I didn't have time to learn how to get on the gain control and adjust accordingly.

The Iron Condor Is Defined

The Iron Condor is an extended options trading built by two other separate dispersed industries - the bulls eye spread and the bear could spread.

Map:

The broad bull is neutral for bull trading. It is constructed by selling or registering one set at a strike price (probably lower than the current share price) and then buying more puts at a lower strike price. Because the put you sell costs more than the put you buy, the transaction results in a net credit.

This net premium income is your maximum profit and can be maintained in full until the shares close above or below the exercise price of the original put you sold.

Iron Condor combines these two condors and collects net premium income from two sources instead of just one. The iron condor is a predestined trading zone with borders up and down. If the shares close in this particular range at the time of expiration, the maximum profit is achieved, which can be quite lucrative based on the total percentage of venture capital.

Below is a graphical representation of Iron Condor strategy for the sake of clarity.

Graph 6

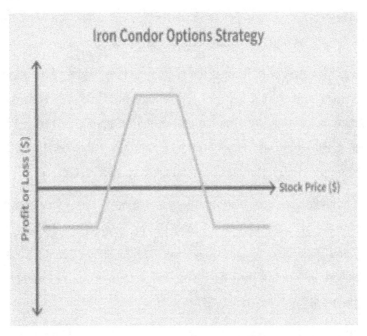

An example of Iron Condor Case

[Note: Committees are excluded from the following example.]

Let's say XYZ is trading at $35 per share, and you don't expect the percentages to be much higher or lower in the short term. You decide to set an iron condor spread, where all options expire in a month.

You also sell a put of $32.50 for $1 and buy a put of $30 for $0.50. Because each contract represents 100 shares of the underlying shares, you will receive an exclusive bonus of $50. This creates a bull section of the iron condor.

On the other side of the transaction, you will simultaneously sell a $37.50 call for $1 and buy a $40 call for $0.50. Multiplying each contract by the 100 underlying shares it represents will give you an additional net bonus of $50. This creates the supporting part of the iron condor.

You have withdrawn $100 in net premium. As long as XYZ closes somewhere between $32.50 per share and $37.50 per share, all options expire worthlessly, and you get a maximum profit of $100

Your maximum loss will occur if the shares are closed after expiration, at or below $30 (maximum bull loss), or at or above $40 (maximum bearish loss). The maximum damage for Iron Condor is the difference in Strike Price for Eliminated Bull or Talk Time 100 (per contract - the number of shares representing the contract) minus the total net bonus received.

In the example above, the maximum loss is $250 (the difference between the exercise prices on both legs) minus the $100 net bonus collected or a total of $150. Even if you have made two legs, because the shares cannot close above $40 per share and below $30 per share, the maximum loss is limited to the betting prices of only one foot.

Iron condors can be a great way to get a high bond yield. However, they are not without risk. An individual trader considering iron condor is advised to conduct further research and consider all risks before trading. Finally, considering that Iron condor strategy has inherent protection from losing your funds completely, it's recommendable for beginners.

Long Iron Butterfly Strategy

The Long Iron Butterfly is another trading strategy and variation on the Iron Condor. Both strategies use a combination of two credit spreads that go in opposite directions, one using calls and the other puts. The difference between the two is the range of bet prices used - Iron Condor has four different bet prices and uses the "out of money" options of the "body" of the set, while Iron Butterfly focuses on using the same "for money" has short (i.e., sold) bet prices. Prizes for the "body" and two long "out of money" options "wings."

As a result, Iron Butterfly gives more credit t hanks to the ATM options sold but also carries a higher risk of the shares falling into the wings, as they tend to be closer to the current trading price of the underlying shares at the time of entry.

Properties of the Iron Butterfly

Limited Risk: Your risk is the difference between ONE of the best prices on each side of the median bet prices (the "body" of the butterfly), the LESS premium you received by selling for; cash calls, and puts institutions. If options trading volatility benefits you, this risk may be minimal.

Limited Reward: Your winnings are limited to the bonus you earn when selling options "for money."

Collateral required: For a credit spread, you usually need to use enough money in your trading account to cover the difference between the exercise prices and the number of shares covered by the option contracts. However, as one of your positions may not be earned after the expiration date, some brokers may take this into account and allow you to allocate only the funds needed to cover one side of the spread.

Recommended Strategy

First, identify the stocks that you think will be delimited by the expiration date of your Iron Butterfly position.

To understand the idea of long iron butterfly strategy better, check out the graph below.

Graph 5

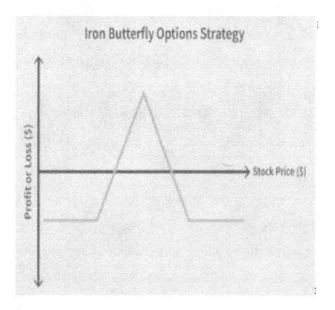

However, if the price of the underlying asset rises in both directions and violates external realizable costs, you can do one of the following two things. Either you leave the position to make sure you don't get the underlying stock, or depending on where you think the stock might go from there, you can take advantage of a nice credit spread feature and lose the position for later maturity. In contrast the other side of the credit spread decreases without risk.

Calendar Put

When an investor sells a near-term put contract, then purchase a second put with prolonged expiration, it is referred to as the calendar put technique. It is simple enough for beginners and can be useful for the professionals. Most strategists apply calendar put when the long-term outlook is bearish, and the short-term outlook stands bullish or neutral. As an investor, you need the underlying price to shift higher or sideways in the subsequent six weeks and decline before the three months.

This options trading technique involves making a premium payment to begin the position provided the two options contracts possess a similar strike price. Essentially, put calendar benefits from time delay considering that the options hold the same strike. Thus, no intrinsic value is available to capture. A calendar put variant entails writing another short-term option contract roll the technique forward once the current term expires. From there, the trader can keep it until the underlying asset shifts considerably, or the expiration of the long-term option is due.

Graph 11

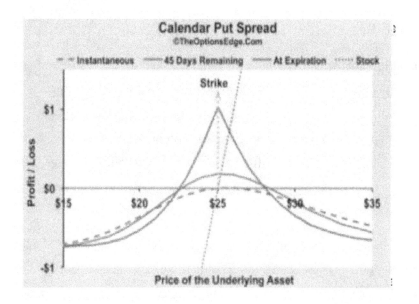

An Example of Calendar Put Strategy

Suppose a trader purchased a 2-month put contract holding a strike price of $100 for $3. Then, he sold a 1-month put bearing the same strike price for $2. A difference between the strike price and the net premium received will give the maximum gain - $100 – ($3 - $2) = $99. In this case, $1 is the maximum loss.

However, if the stock trades at the strike price on the due date of the near-term option, the maximum gain occurs. The option will expire worthlessly, and the investor will have long put only. In a situation where the stock declines to zero prior to the due date, the investor can sell the stock for $100. Thus, a maximum gain of $99 will be realized.

Diagonal Put

A combination of a short calendar put spread, and vertical put spreads make up a diagonal put spread. Thus, this strategy often exhibits the attributes of both spreads. Among such attributes include directionally bearish and short volatility with minimal, zero, or positive time decay. The resultant time decay will depend on the selected expirations and strike price. Below is a graphical representation of the relationship between the strike price of the underlying asset and profit/loss in relation to the expiration date.

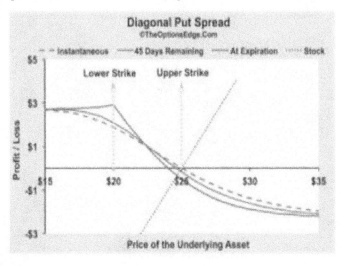

To use this strategy, you need to take a bearish position in stock using options. However, it's vital to take an approach with less time decay compared to a traditional vertical put spread. In comparison to long-dated options, short-dated ones usually decay faster. Consequently, a diagonal put spread possesses a less time decay compared to a vertical put spread. However, the similarity between diagonal put spread and vertical put spread is that they utilize various strike prices to get a directional movement.

When you use a diagonal put spread, the maximum gain will be the difference between the higher strike and lower strike, then subtracted from the premium received. In a situation where the market goes against your strategy, the maximum loss will occur.

Chapter 8

Bull and Bear Call Spread

Bull Call Spread

You must have picked up so far that wherever there are bears, there are also bulls, at least in the stock market jungle.

If an investor is very "bullish" about a stock, he will tend to buy a simple call option. He thus benefits leveraged and unlimited from the upward movement of the share. If it is wrong, or if the stock does not move up fast enough, it will lose its stake at most. You should note that even a rising share will not rise immeasurably in a certain period. If you have a bullish view of a stock and expect it to hit a certain price target. In options jargon, the bull call spread is sometimes called Long Call spread or debit call spread.

Structure of the Bull Call Spread

This strategy consists of buying a call option, which is usually out of the money (whose base price is above the current share price) and selling a call option, which is also out of the money, and whose base price is higher than the base price purchased call Option lies. The structure of a bull call is, therefore, the exact reflection of a bear call spread. Both options of a bull call have the same expiry date. The Bull Call Spread summarized:

- Long call with base price A
- Short call with base price B

The share price is usually below the base price A. Both options have the same expiry date (this is called a vertical debit spread)

Profile of a bull call

Principle of the Bull Call Spread

The bull call is an alternative to a simple long call. In addition to buying a base price a call option, sell a cheaper base price B call option to lower your trade costs. This will reduce your total stake and your maximum risk of loss. Due to the price difference between the two options, you always pay an amount as a debit when opening this position. By selling the call option, this amount is lower than if you were only buying a long call. In return, your potential profit in the case of a strong upward movement is lower than with a simple call option. You will expect that the share price ideally rises to base price B.

Tips for Trading Bull Call Spreads

• The profit and loss profile is identical to the profile of a bull put spread. The main difference is the cash flow when opening the position. The

Bull Call Spread requires a cash amount (debit) upon entry. The profit comes from the closure. The bull put spread gives a premium (credit) when entering the position. There is a "buyback" clause when you exit.

Who And When Is The Bull Call Spread Suitable For?

This strategy is intended for traders who already have experience in options trading. The execution of the bull call spread is not particularly complicated, but it does require a certain amount of expertise in the selection of base prices and a good estimate of the price movement of the underlying over a certain period. You open Bull Call if you expect the underlying stock to rise and if you have a target price for that stock. This target price would be, for example, the base price B of the call option sold.

This strategy pays off when the stock price expires above the upper base price A of the purchased call option plus the amount paid for the trade.

Maximum profit = difference between base prices - paid debit.

The way you choose the two strike prices determines the maximum return potential and the maximum risk. Partial profit is achieved if the share price is above the breakeven point. Bull Call does not have to be held until the options expire. You can close out the position early and take the profits (or losses) with you.

The Advantages and Disadvantages of the Bull Call Spread In A Nutshell

Advantages:

- Bull Call is less than a simple call.
- Depending on the choice of base prices, the possible returns of Bull Call are very high.
- The risk is limited.

Disadvantages:

- The maximum profit is limited, and the position does not benefit from a continuous increase in the share.
- Time is running against you: the stock has to rise in a certain period to make a profit.

Example of Bull Call on Disney stock

For example, suppose that Disney (DIS) stock is currently trading at $ 129. To implement the Bull Call Spread strategy, a trader buys a call option and simultaneously sells another call option at high price and with the same expiry date. The short call (the short-selling call option) with a term of 78 days has a base price (strike) of $ 135 and is sold short at $ 3.20.

Long Call (the purchased call option) with the same term has a base price of $ 130 and is bought at $ 5.45. The amount (the debit) that the trader has to pay for this trade is ($ 5.45 - $ 3.20) x 100 = $ 225. That is also the maximum risk of loss. The breakeven position is 130 $ + 2.25 $ = 132.25 $. Above this rate, the trader starts making profits. If the stock price is above $ 135 at the end of the term of the options, the profit for the trader is $ 275.

Bear Call Spread

Making profits when the markets go up is relatively easy. Still making money when the markets fall requires more skill and knowledge of trading techniques that most investors may not be very familiar with. The bear call spread is one of the combinations of options that benefit from falling stock markets and even contain a security cushion should the markets rise again. In options jargon, the bear call spread is sometimes called the short call spread or credit call spread.

Structure of the bear call spread

This strategy consists of short selling a call option that is out of the money (whose base price is above the current share price) and buying a call option that is also out of the money and whose base price is higher than the base price sold called option. Both options have the same expiry date. The Bear Call Spread summarized:

- Short call with base price A
- Long call with base price B

The share price is usually below the base price A and both options have the same expiry date (this is called a vertical spread)

Profile of a bear call spread

Principle of the Bear Call Spread

With a bear call spread, you are obliged to sell the share at strike price A if the short option is exercised. You also have the right to buy the share at base price B. A bear call is an alternative to a simple short call. In addition to selling a strike price a call option, buy a cheaper strike price call option B to limit your risk if the stock rises. Due to the price difference between the two options, the investor always receives a premium (credit) when opening this position. By purchasing the call option, this net income (your premium) is lower than with the simple short call strategy. The purchased call option protects you against higher losses in the event of a strong upward movement.

You will expect that the share price will stay below base price A and that both options will expire worthlessly. In this case, you do not have to pay transaction fees to close your position. A Bear Call Spread is very easy to implement. Ideally, you buy one call option and sell the other call option at the same time as part of an option combination.

Tips for Trading Bear Call Spreads

• For a bear call spread, I would recommend choosing strike price A of the short option so that it is at least one standard deviation or more from the current stock price. This increases your likelihood of success. However, the farther away the base price is, the lower the premium you collect. Options with a delta of 16 correspond to a standard deviation. Ideally, this base price is close to a solid resistance in terms of chart technology.

• Prefer short maturities because the options lose value faster in the last 60 days before their expiry date. This loss of time value is an advantage for you as the seller of the options. See also our article on the subject of declining fair value.

Who And When Is Bear Call Spread Suitable For?

This strategy is intended for traders who already have experience in options trading. The Bear Call Spread is not particularly complicated to execute, but it does require a certain amount of expertise in the choice of base prices and a good understanding of the maximum risk of the position taken. You open a bear call spread if you expect the stock to fall, move sideways, or rise slightly. The underlying share may rise to base price A without reducing the maximum profit (the premium). Ideally, an entry should take place at a time when the underlying stock exhibits a high level of implied volatility. As a result, the options are more expensive, and a higher premium can be collected accordingly.

This strategy pays off if the share price on expiry is below the upper strike price if the short-sold call option plus the premium received.

The Advantages and Disadvantages of the Bear Call Spread In A Nutshell

Advantages:

- The Bear Call Spread achieves the maximum profit in 3 possible scenarios: a sideways movement, a downward movement, and a slight upward movement of the underlying stock.
- The risk is limited.
- The bear call spread benefits from the decline in implied volatility.
- The bear call spread benefits from the decline in fair value.

Disadvantages:

- The maximum profit is limited, and the position accordingly does not benefit from a continuous fall in the share.
- Depending on the choice of the base price, only a small upward movement of the share price is permitted to remain in the profit zone.

Example: Bear Call Spreads on Chevron (Ticker: CVX)

For example, suppose that Chevron (CVX) stock is currently trading at $ 115. To implement the Bear Call Spread strategy, a trader sells a call option and buys a call option with high price at the same expiry date. The short call (the short-sold call option) with a term of 53 days has a base price (strike) of $ 120 and is sold short at $ 2.00. Long Call (the purchased call option) with the same term has a base price of $ 125 and is bought at $ 0.70. The total premium received by the trader is ($ 2.00 - $ 0.70) x 100 = $ 130.

The break-even position is 120 $ + 1.30 $ = 121.30 $. Above this rate, the trader starts making losses. If the stock price is below $ 120 at the end of the term of the options, the profit for the trader is $ 130. This is the premium that was initially collected. The position margin requirement would be: ($ 125 - $ 120) x $ 100 - $ 130 = $ 370. It also corresponds to the maximum loss of position. The return on the bear call spread would, therefore, be $ 130 / $ 370 = 35.1% in 53 days.

Chapter 9

Choosing a Broker

For selecting brokers, you have many options available. There is full service, discount, online, etc. Understanding the differences between them and selecting the ones best suited for your purposes is crucial if you wish to succeed. Another area that a lot of beginners ignore and then receive a rude lesson in is the regulations surrounding options trading.

There aren't too many rules to comply with, but they have significant consequences for your capital and risk strategies.

Choosing a Broker

Generally, there are two major varieties of brokers: Discount and full service. In fact, a lot of full-service brokers have discount arms these days so that you will see some overlap. Full service refers to an organization where brokerage is just a part of a larger financial supermarket.

The broker might offer you other investment solutions, estate planning strategies, and so on. They'll also have an in-house research wing, which will send you reports to help you trade better. Besides this, they'll also have phone support in case you have questions or wish to place an order.

Once you develop a good relationship with them, a full-service broker will become a good organization to network. Every broker loves a profitable customer since it helps with marketing. A full-service broker will have good relationships in the industry, and if you have specific needs, they can put you in touch with the right people.

The price of all this service is you paying higher commissions than average.

It is up to you to see whether this is a good price for you to pay. You need not sign up with a full-service broker to trade successfully. Order matching is done electronically, so it's not as if a person on the floor can get you a better price these days. Therefore, a full-service house will not give you better execution.

Discount brokers, on the other hand, are all about focus. They help you trade and that is it. They will not advise, at least not intentionally, from a business perspective, and phone ordering is nonexistent. That doesn't mean they reduce customer service. Far from it.

Commissions will be lower as well, far lower than what you can expect to pay at a full-service house. The downside of a discount brokerage is that you will not receive any particular product recommendations or solutions outside of your speculative activities. Many people prefer to trade (using a separate account) with the broker they have their retirement accounts with; they keep so everything in-house.

So, which one should you choose? Well, if you aim to keep costs as low as possible, then select a discount broker. In fact, only where you're keen on keeping things in one place should you choose a full-service broker. These days, there's no difference between the two options otherwise.

An exception here is if you have a sizeable amount of capital, worth of half a million dollars. In such cases, a full-service broker will be cheaper because of their volume-based commission offers. You'll pay the same rate or as close to what a discount broker would charge you, and you get all the additional services. Whatever additional amounts you need to invest can be handled by the firm through their wealth management line of business.

There are a few terms you must understand, no matter which broker you choose, so let's look at these now.

Margin

Margin refers to the number of assets you currently hold in your account. Your assets are cash and positions. As the market value of your positions fluctuates, so does the amount of margin you have. Margin is an important concept to grasp since it is at the core of your risk management discipline.

When you open an account with your broker, you will have a choice to make. You can open either a cash or margin account. To trade options, open a margin account. Briefly, a cash account does not include leverage within it, so all you can trade are stocks. There are no account minimums for a cash account, and even if they are, they're minuscule.

A margin account, on the other hand, is subject to weird rules. First, the minimum balances for a margin account are higher. Most brokers will impose a $10,000 minimum, and some will even increase this amount based on your trading style. The account minimum achieves nothing by itself, but it acts as a commitment of sorts for the broker.

The thinking is that with this much money on the line, the person trading will be more serious about it and won't blow it away. If only it worked like that. Anyway, the minimum balance is a hard and fast rule. Another rule you should know is the Pattern Day Trader (PDT) designation.

PDT is a rule that comes directly from the SEC. We classify anyone who executes four or more orders within five days as a PDT ("Pattern Day Trader," 2019). Once this tag is slapped onto you, your broker will ask you to post at least $25,000 in the margin as a minimum balance. Again, this minimum balance does nothing, but the SEC figures that if you screw up, this gives you enough of a buffer.

Each strategy by itself plays out over a month or more, so once you enter, all you need to do is monitor it, and you can adjust it. However, if you will avoid the PDT, you're limited to entering just three positions per workweek.

My advice is to study the strategies and to start slowly. Trade only one instrument at first and see how it goes and then expand once you gain more confidence. At that point, you'll have enough experience to figure out how much capital you need. Remember that even exiting a position is considered a trade, so PDT doesn't refer just to trade entry.

Margin Call

One other aspect of margin you must understand is the margin call. This is a dreaded message for most traders, including institutional ones. The purpose of all risk management is to keep you as far away as possible from this ever happening to you. A margin call is issued when you have inadequate funds in your account to cover its requirements.

Remember that your margin is the combination of the cash you hold plus the value of your positions. If you have $1000 in cash, but your position is currently in a loss of -$900, you'll receive a margin call to post more cash to cover the potential loss you're headed for. In fact, you'll receive it well in advance. If you don't post more margins, your broker has the right to close out your positions and recover whatever cash they can to stop their risk limits from being triggered.

The threshold beyond which your broker will issue a margin call is called the maintenance margin. Usually, you need to maintain 25% of your initial position value (that is when you enter a position) as cash in your account. Most brokers have a handy indicator that tells you how close you are to the limit.

The leading cause of margin calls is leverage. With a margin account, you can borrow money from your broker and use that to boost your returns. Let's look at an example: if you trade with $10,000 of your own money and borrow $20,000 from your broker to enter a position, you control $30,000 worth of the position. Let's say this position makes a gain of $10,000 to bring its total value to $40,000.

You've just made a 100% return on this investment (since you invested only $10,000) despite the total return on the position is 33% (10,000/30,000).

What happens if you lose $10,000 on the position, though? Well, you just lost 100% despite the position losing only 33%. Leverage is a double-edged sword.

It is far too simplistic to call leverage bad or good. It is what it is. If you're a beginner, you should not be borrowing money to trade under any circumstances. When you're experienced, you can do so as much as you want. Please note I'm differentiating between the leverage where you borrow money, and the leverage options provide.

With options, a single contract gives you control over a larger pie of stock, but the option premium still needs to be paid. It is, therefore, cheaper to trade options than the common stock. If you were to borrow money to pay for the option premium, then you're indulging in foolish behavior, and you need to step away.

There's a difference between leverage being inherent within the structure of the instrument and using leverage to increase the amount of something you can buy. The latter when you're a beginner.

Execution

A favorite pastime of unsuccessful traders is to complain about execution. Their losses are always the broker's fault, and if it weren't for the greedy brokers, they'd be rolling in the dough, diving in and out of it like Scrooge McDuck. Complaining about your execution will get you nothing. A big reason for these complaints is that most beginner traders don't realize that the price they see on the screen is not the same as what is being traded on the exchange.

We live in an era of high-frequency trading, and the markets' smallest measurement of time has gone from second to microseconds. Trades are constantly pouring in, and the matching engine is always finding suitable sellers for buyers. Given the pace of the market, it is important to understand that it is impossible to figure out the exact price of an instrument.

Therefore, within your risk management plan, you must make allowance for times of high volatility when the fluctuations will be bigger. For now, I want you to understand that just because the price you received differed from what was on screen doesn't mean the broker is incompetent.

How do you identify an incompetent broker? Customer service and the quality of the trading terminal they give you access to are the best indicators. Your broker is not in the game to trade against you or fleeces you. Admittedly, this is not the case with FX, but we're not discussing FX in this book. So, stop blaming your broker and look at your systems instead, assuming the broker passes basic due diligence.

For placing orders with your broker, you have many options. There are different order types you can place, and each order has a specific purpose. First off, we have the market order. This is the simplest order to understand.

When you place a market order, you're telling your broker to fill your entire order at whatever price they can find on the market.

A market order results in fast fills unless there's a volatility event of some sort going on. The next type of order you can place is the limit order. The limit prioritizes order price over quantity. For example, if you want to enter 100 units of an instrument at $10, your broker will buy as much as possible under or equal to $10. If they can get just 90 units under $10, then that's it.

Chapter 10

Financial Leverage

Financial Leverage

The process of using borrowed capital (debt) to increase the shareholder's return on their investments or equity in capital structure is called financial leverage or Trading on equity. The financial leverage analyzed by the firm is intended to earn more return on the fixed charge funds rather than their costs. The surplus will increase the return on the owner's equity whereas the deficit will decrease the return on the owner's equity. Financial leverage affects the EPS (Earnings per share). When the EBIT increases, then EPS increases.

For example, if the firm borrows a debt from creditors for $1000 at 7% interest per annum i.e. $70 and invests this debt to earn a 12% return on this i.e. $120 per annum. Then the difference of surplus i.e. $50 which is after interest payment done to the creditors of the firm will belong to the shareholders or owners of the firm and it is referred to as profit from financial leverage. Conversely, if the firm would earn a 5% return, then the firm has a loss of $20 (i.e. $70 - $50) to the shareholders.

Highly leveraged companies may be at risk of bankruptcy if they are unable to make a payment on their debt, but it can increase shareholder's return on their investment and there are tax advantages associated with leverage.

Financial leverage ratio = EBIT / EBT

The financial leverage ratio is used to analyses the Capital structure and financial risk of the company. It explains how the fixed interest-bearing loan capital affects the operating profit of the firm. If EBIT is more than EBT, this ratio becomes more than 1.

Types of Leverages

- Operating Leverage

Operating leverage is just concerned with the investment activities of an individual firm. It is about the incurrence of the fixed cost of operation in a company's income stream. The operating price can either be fixed, semi-fixed, variable as well as semi-variable. The fixed fee is contractual, and it is subject to time. It does not necessarily have to change when the sales change, and it is supposed to be paid despite the number of sales.

- Financial Leverage

It is a relation to the combination of debts as well as equity in the capital format of a company. When there are financial charges in existence, the financial leverage will as well exist. The business costs should not depend on the operating profits in any way. The sources in which the funds that help to boost an investment come from can be put in categories. The funds can either be having a fixed charge, and some may not be having the fixed financial cost. Debentures, preference shares, bonds as well as long-term loans have a fixed financial burden. Equity shares are known to have no fixed charge at all.

- Combined Leverage

If you bring both the operating leverage and the financial leverage together, they will come up with the combined force. It is concerning the risk of one not being able to cover up for the total amount of the fixed charges. When a firm can cover fully on the operating as well as the financial burdens that is when the term combined leverage comes in. The higher the fixed operating cost as well as the financial charges, the higher the level of the combined force.

- Working Capital Leverage

When there is a decrease in the investment of a particular asset, there will be an increase in profit. When there are many investors in the market and dealing with the same trade, there will be decreased profit. When there is a decrease in the investment of an asset, the risk associated with it will go high. That means that risks, as well as returns, have direct relations. When the probability of risk goes up, there is a likely hood that the profit will increase as well. The ability of an individual firm to increase the effect of the change in the current stock on the firm's returns is working capital leverage. It is so when there is an assumption that the liabilities are constant.

The Risks of Incorrect Use

Limited Growth

When you have a loan, the lending company will expect that you will pay in the period that was agreed upon when you were getting the loan. They hope that you will be on time and no failures should come along the way. It is a problem when an investor borrows money for a long-term project that will not generate some income immediately. That will make them find an alternative to how they will pay the loan to avoid breaching the contract. If the payment period has come, and the investor has no returns, paying the mortgage can be a burden in one way or the other. When you decide to start paying the loan, it will mean that you use the money you borrowed to pay back. When that happens, you will have less money for financing your operations. You will not be in a position to implement full on the plan that you had. That means that you can have retardation, and you will not execute your plan fully. When investing, you need a plan and to set deadlines for the completion so that you will remain on your focus. When you have to pay the loan with the money that you borrowed, you will not be in a position to hit your deadlines. That will mean that you will experience limited growth, and you may not have the potential to continue as per the plan.

Losing Assets

When you are unable to pay loans, and you are highly leveraged, that can lead to a conspirator of the assets that you have. There is no way that a company should pay capital sourcing from equity. When that happens, and the lender expects that you will pay your loan in time, they can decide to take some of your assets to stand in for the loan. The assets can be of a similar value or a value higher than your investment. When in a loan, the company is supposed to pay the lender before any other deductions. Repossession of assets can happen if there is no money to pay the lender in time. It the lender has to be paid even before the employees of the company, it means that the employees may look for another option and quit working with you. That will make you lose assets of value, and you will be left stranded.

Inability to Get More Financing

Before a lender gives you money to invest in any trade, they will first check out whether you have any other loan. They will do that to establish how secure their payment is with you. If you are in debt, no lender will want to lend you more because they are not sure whether you will be in a position to clear their debt. They will access the risk that is associated in case the company goes down, meaning there will be no one to pay their loan. When a company goes down, it is declared bankrupt, and that means that the lender cannot claim their money even on a legal basis. No lender will agree to put them last on your loan list since they know they will be the last to be paid.

An Investor Will Not Be in a Position to Attract Equity

When a company has high leverage, they are not able to increase the equity capital amount. And it is rare for an investor to give money to a business that has bid records of unclear loans. In the same way, lenders will avoid providing more money to a company with high amounts of investments, and the same way investors avoid such business. You will lose the potential of attracting investors when you have a lot of pending debts. When a lender knows they are the last in your line to be paid their loan, they will not find it comfortable to lend you. If at with any chance you get an investor to give you, they will demand a significant percentage in terms of ownership in return of borrowing you the money.

Advantages of Leverage

Increase in Profit

Leverage will earn you more benefits without necessarily having to put in more effort. Since it is borrowed money, you do not have to toil so much so that you can earn it; instead, you look for a lender. When you fulfill the requirements, the lender will finance you and you will have to repay back when the period lapses. When you inject more capital into a business, it is likely to give you more returns under favorable market conditions.

An Increase in Capital Efficiency

When you increase the amount of money in a particular transaction can lead to a rise in productivity on how you use your capital. You need to consider capital as an asset, and it can increase the level of yields. When you take a loan, you will increase the amount of money, and you will raise the level of efficiency.

Is a Tool that Mitigates Against Low Volatility?

Leverage is a great approach that can be put in place to mitigate the effect brought about by low volatility. Volatile trade is known to deliver huge profits in the Forex trade. It can deliver good benefits from a small transaction and can shield against the effect that comes with low volatility. A small entity can become a big firm with the help of leverage. Leverage will help you to capitalize on the small significant levels of movement in the trading price.

Disadvantages of Leverage

Lower Liquidity

It is worth noting that a lot of individual stock options dint has many volumes. There are cases where one is forced to own very few stocks. The aspect that in all the options that one has will trade at different strikes of payments as well as expectations, the particular option will be forced to have a less volume unless it is one of the most popular stock index or stocks.

High Spreads

The art of lacking liquidity among these trading options causes higher spreads. The aspect is detrimental due to the fact that one is forced to pay more indirect costs while using thus trade option. The element is linked to the fact that when one is using the opportunity, they will be spreading the trade

Higher Commissions

When one is operating with such organizations, one is forced to pay using commission terms. In other words, one has to pay a certain amount of commission for each dollar that is invested. The demerit is worsened by the fact that the option has very many options that forced one to have a lot of spreads.

Chapter 11

What Are "The Greeks"

One of the things you need to learn about and be aware of when it comes to options trading is the "Greeks." These are parameters with Greek letters that will help you estimate the future behavior of options pricing. So, you need to keep them in mind when considering getting into a trade and exiting your trades. There are five of these parameters in total. They are delta, theta, gamma, rho, and Vega. In most cases, delta and theta are what you need to pay attention to, and the rest are details. As we will see, in today's environment where interest rates are low and not changing by very much, rho isn't of much relevance. But, of course, you should be aware of what rho means because, at some point in the future, interest rates may rise higher or become more volatile.

Vega has some relevance in relation to the volatility of a stock. Most of the time, it's not that important, but as we'll see, there are certain situations when it can impact options prices significantly, and there are strategies that you can use to profit from this.

For the most part, options traders need to be focused on delta and theta. Understanding these two parameters can help you be more aware and effective in your options trading. They will help you to be more informed when it comes to the prospects of a given options contract, and where it is going once you've invested in it. A more informed trader is always going to be a more successful trader, and those who do their trading on the fly are usually the same people that end up with heavy losses.

Delta

The first Greek that we are going to look at is one of the most important. The main piece of information that you are going to get from the delta is the amount that the price of an option is going to change in reaction to the given change of the underlying stock's price. Delta is expressed as a fraction, so it can be viewed as giving you the percentage by which the price of the option will change as a fraction of the change in the stock price. Or you can just look at it in terms of change by a dollar in the stock's price.

Looking at a $235 strike call option on Apple, the delta is 0.5427. So that means there is going to be about a 54 cent change in the price of the option for every dollar price change in Apple stock. You will recall that earlier; we mentioned that there is a rule of thumb for an at the money option – it will change by 50 cents for every dollar change in the price of the underlying stock. This proves the point that the option is about $1 in the money, which is barely in the money – and it's going to change by 54 cents, which is quite close to the 50 cent value.

Delta is not a fixed value. You will see it change in real-time as the stock price moves up and down. Of course, in most circumstances, the delta is not going to change very much over a relatively short time period, like a day or so. But you need to be aware that when you go look up the delta and see that it is a specific value, that value is dynamic and not fixed, so you need to keep your eye on how it's changing.

Theta

The second Greek that you want to pay close attention to is called theta. This gives you a relatively precise estimate of the time decay of the option. Theta is expressed as a negative value, which is an indication that it will decrease in value for each passing day. Theta is dynamic like delta, but it will be changing by small amounts in the entire day of trading as long as there is a change in the value of the price of the stock. The main point at which theta becomes important is with turnover. That is, options prices drop at market open due to value lost through time decay. And guess how much they drop? Take theta and multiply it by 100. So, if theta is -0.11, that means that the price of the option is going to automatically drop by $11 when the market opens the next day.

Theta is going to have higher values, the closer the option is to be at the money. Theta has smaller values when options are more in the money, but it also has smaller values when options are more out of the money.

But rather than worrying about the variation, you need to be aware of the value of the theta for any option that you invest in. This way, you can take into account the amount of money you are going to lose if you hold any option overnight.

This will have to be considered along with many other factors, of course. But, in some cases, it is not going to be worth it to hold the option overnight and take the hit to the options price. If you have an option that is trading at $100, a theta value of -0.11 means that your option is going to lose 11% of its value overnight. Is that significant? It depends since a movement in share price can easily overwhelm that value. If you were trading call options, and the share price was to go up by 50 cents, with delta equal to say 0.65 that would indicate that the option's price would go up by $32.50 from the delta but drop by $11 from the theta. So, on the net, you'd be profiting. That means both values need to be taken into account, and you need to be on top of things as far as estimating how the stock is going to move.

Earlier, we mentioned that beginning options traders often make the mistake of holding losing trades all the way through expiration, and they end up losing their entire investment when they could have cut their losses. But there is another problem many beginning traders run into – and that is getting out too early when they should not do so. The above example might illustrate this, believe it or not, many new options traders will panic at the thought of time decay, and sell their option before market close, and then the following morning even though the option starts out of the gate taking a hit because of the time decay-driven losses, it quickly recovers and becomes profitable due to a move in the underlying stock price.

Vega

The underlying volatility of a stock is an important factor influencing options prices. Volatility is a measure of how drastically stock prices are changing with time. If a stock has a median share price of $32, and it fluctuates between $30 and $34 over the course of a week, it is far less volatile than a stock that has a median share price of $32, but the second stock fluctuates between $25 and $50 over the same time period. So, volatility is a measure of how much change there is in a share price and how frequently it's changing. You can think of this in terms of graphics as well. A very jagged curve fluctuating up and down between wildly different values is very volatile, while a stable stock price that is practically a smooth line over the same time period is not very volatile.

One measure you can look for on your brokerage account or stock market sites is to look up the value of beta for a given company. Beta is a comparison of the stock's volatility relative to the market average. It is expressed as being greater or less than 1. The stock market average is normalized to 1.0. Any value greater than 1.0 indicates a highly volatile stock, while a value of less than 1.0 indicates a stock that is not very volatile.

If you look up a given stock, and you find that beta is 1.53 that means it's 53% more volatile than the market average. On the other hand, if you look up a stock and find that beta is 0.4 that means its only 40% as volatile as the average. Beta is actually calculated using five-year averages.

The volatility of a stock really doesn't have anything to do with whether or not the stock is desirable to own as an investment. Some very highly desirable stocks have high beta values, but some have relatively low beta values.

Gamma

Gamma is one of the Greeks that get less attention, and it's a little more complicated, which might be one of the reasons that it's not tops on most people's lists. The value of paying much attention to it is not as clear cut either. Gamma is a quantity that gives you the rate of change of delta. It will tell you the amount of change in the value of delta you can expect when the stock price changes. Gamma values tend to be pretty small, on the order of 0.01-0.03 or so. For example, let the share price be $100, delta 0.65, and gamma 0.01. If the share price were to rise $1 that would mean that delta would rise to 0.66. If gamma had been 0.03, then the value of delta would have changed to 0.68 for the same $1 change in the share price.

Rho

The last of the Greeks is rho. We are leaving that to the end because these days, Rho is the least important of the Greeks. Rho is related to interest rates. Specifically, the value of rho is related to a hypothetical "risk-free" interest rate. It gives you an estimate of how the option's price would change relative to a one-point change in the risk-free interest rate. Since interest rates are not changing by large amounts in today's environment, this is not going to be a quantity that is going to require much attention.

So, what is the risk-free interest rate? This is an estimate of what the interest rate would be if you had your money in a risk-free investment. Interest rates for the past ten years have been at historic lows. Generally, the risk-free interest rate is taken to be the interest rate on a 10-year U.S. Treasury. That is about as close as you can get to a risk-free investment. You are pretty much guaranteed, at least for the time being, of getting your capital back if you invest in ten year U.S. government bonds.

Chapter 12

Tips for Beginners

When Trading Options, Watch Out For Earnings Release Dates

Call and put options are generally expensive with the price increases significantly if there is an earnings release announcement looming. The reason is that the anticipation of very good or very bad earnings report will likely affect the stock price. When this is an underlying stock in an options trade, then you should adjust your trades appropriately.

Once an earnings release has been made, then options prices will fall significantly. You need to also watch out very carefully for this. The prices will first go up just before the earnings release and then fall shortly thereafter. It is also possible for call options prices to dip despite earnings announcements. This may happen if the earnings announced are not as impressive as expected.

As an example, stocks such as Google may rise insanely during the earnings announcement week only to dip significantly shortly thereafter. Consider Apple shares that were trading at $450 at the markets. Call options with Apple as the underlying stock were trading at $460. However, the market had targeted a price of $480 within 3 days, which did not happen. This cost investors' money. Such underlying assets are considered volatile due to the high increase in price, rapid drop shortly thereafter and related risk of losing money.

If You Are Dealing With Call and Put Options, Embrace the Underlying Stock's Trend

As an investor and trader in options, you need to consider the trend of the underlying stock as your friend. This means that you should not fight it. Basically, if the stock price is headed upwards, you should find a strategy that is in tandem with this movement. If you oppose it, you are unlikely to win.

Similarly, if the stock is on a downward trend, then do not oppose this movement but try and find a strategy that will accommodate this trend. You need to understand, however, that this saying is intended to guide you but is not necessarily a rule. This means that you apply it even while you consider all other factors. For instance, the major news may have an immediate effect on the price trend of a stock or shares.

As a trader, you should learn to jump successfully on a trend and follow the crowds rather than go to extremes and oppose it. Most amateurs who see an upward trend often think the stock is about to level out. However, the reality is that the momentum is often considered a great thing by seasoned traders. Therefore, do not try and oppose the trend because you will surely lose. Instead, try and design a strategy that will accommodate the trend. In short, the trend is always your friend, do not resist, and momentum is truly great.

Find Out the Breakeven Point before Buying Your Options

Now, you need to identify a call option that you wish to invest in, especially after studying its performance on the market. Before buying, however, you should work out the breakeven point. In order to find this breakeven point, you will have to consider things such as the commissions charged and the bid spread.

It is very important that you are positive that the underlying stock of your options will move sufficiently so as to surpass the breakeven point and earn a tidy profit. You should, therefore, learn how to work out the breakeven point in options trade.

Calculating the Breakeven Point

As an options trader, you need to know how to calculate and find the breakeven point. In options trading, there are basically 2 break-even points. With short term options, you need to make use of the commission rates and bid spread to work out the breakeven point. This is if you intend to hold on to the options until their expiration date.

Now, if you are seeking short-term trade without holding on to the options, then find out the difference between asking price and bid price. This difference is also known as the spread.

Before Buying a Call or Put Option, Look at the Underlying Stock's Chart

Basically, you want to find out as much information as possible about the performance and worth of an underlying stock before investing in it.

You should, therefore, ensure that you take a serious look at the chart of the stock. This chart should indicate the performance of the stock in the last couple of days. The best is to look at a stock's performance in the last 30 and 90 days. You should also take a look at its last year's performance.

When you look at the charts, look at the movement of the shares and try and note any trends. Also, try and observe any general movement of the shares. Then answer a couple of questions. For instance, is the stock operating within a narrow range? Or is it bending upwards or downwards? Is this chart in tandem with your options trading strategy?

To identify the trend of a particular stock, try and draw a straight line along in the middle of the share prices. Then draw a line both above and below so as to indicate a channel of the general flow of the share.

Chart Readings and Buying Call Options

Let us assume that you wish to invest in a call option. Then you should ask yourself if the stock price is likely to rise and why. If you think that the stock will rise and trade at a higher level, then you may be mistaken, unless something drastic happens or new information becomes evident. New information can be a shareholders' meeting, impending earnings announcement, a new CEO, product launch, and so on.

If there is a chart showing the presence of support at lower prices and stock prices fall to that level, then it may be advisable to buy call options. The call option will be a great bet when prices are down because prices will very likely head back up. However, never allow greed to occupy your mind. When you see a profit, take and do not wait too long.

Chart Readings and Buying Put Options

Now, supposing the stock chart indicates a solid resistance at a higher price. If the stock is beginning to approach this higher level, then it is possible that the price might begin to move in that direction as well. So as the price moves, expect to gain small but significant profits. Avoid greed, so anytime the stock price falls simply move in and make some money.

Chart Readings for Purchase of Call and Put Options

Now, if your chart readings indicate that the shares are within the lower levels of its range, then it is likely that daily changes in price will send it towards the middle of the range. If this is so, then you should move in and make a profit as soon as the price tends upwards. Even minor profits such as buying at $1 and selling at $1.15 mean a 15% profit margin.

The Price of Any Stock Can Move In 3 Basic Directions

These directions are up, down, and no movement at all. Depending on the kind of call that you have, you can leverage this movement to make a profit or at least avoid incurring losses.

Plenty of first-time traders and investors assume that prices of securities will go either up or down. However, this is a wrong school of thought because sometimes there is no movement at all in the price of stocks and shares. This is a very important fact in the world of options trading.

There are plenty of real-life, practical examples that show a particular stock or share which did not move significantly for quite a lengthy period. For instance, the KOL share traded within a $4 range for a total of 23 days. If you had invested money in either a call option or a put option through this stock, you would have lost money.

According to seasoned traders, chances of making a profit with a call or put option are hardly ever 50% but only 33%. This is likely due to the fact that stock price movements are random. You will eventually realize that 33% of the time, stocks rise; 33% of the time, they dip in price; and another 33% of the time, they stay the same. Time will more often be your worst enemy if you have a long put or call option.

A purchase of a call option is usually with the hope that prices will go up. In the event that prices do rise, then you will make a profit. At other times, the prices will remain the same or even fall. In such events, if you have an out-of-the-money call, the option will most likely expire, and you will lose your investment. In the event that the price remains stagnant and you have an in-the-money option, then you will at least recoup some of the money you invested.

There will be some times when frustrations will engulf you. This is when you just sit and watch prices start to skyrocket just a couple of weeks after the options you purchased had expired. This is often an indicator that your strategy was not on point and you did not give it sufficient time. Even seasoned traders sometimes buy call options that eventually expire in a given month and then the stock prices rise sharply in the following month.

It is therefore advisable to purchase a longer-term call option rather than one that expires after a single month. Now, since stocks move in 3 general directions, it is assumed that close to 70% of options, traders with long call and put options suffer losses. On the other hand, this implies that 70% of options sellers make money. This is one of the main reasons why conservative options traders prefer to write or sell options.

Be Wary Of Over Trading

Early on, it is perfectly natural to feel as though the times you are not trading are times that you are actively missing out on potentially significant gains. However, the simple fact of the matter is that the best way to win is sometimes simply not to play which means you need to be critical of the market as a whole because sometimes there really will be simply nothing worth chasing happening at the given time. Keep in mind that, even if you are already steering clear of truly terrible trades, the odds are high that you are still trading far more frequently than the pros. What's more, if most professional traders traded as frequently as the average amateur then they would like to be out on the street after a week. Generally speaking, aim to limit your trading costs to less than two percent of your total portfolio to ensure that your returns remain as high as possible. These tips should be enough to get you started. As time passes by, you will learn what options to look for and what to avoid. Remember that seasoned traders are considered those who have spent years on this business, not just a few months.

Chapter 13

Avoiding Common Pitfalls in Options Trading

All successful options traders go through a learning curve before they start profiting consistently. Some of them put in an all-out effort to learn by spending countless hours reading on the topic or by watching video tutorials. Others learn at a more leisurely pace and once they get a grip of the basics, they lean more towards learning from their own experience. Irrespective of the type of learner you are, one way to cut short that learning curve is by learning from the mistakes of others.

1. Buying Naked Options without Hedging

This is one of the most fundamental mistakes made by amateur options traders and is also one of the costliest ones that could make them go broke in no time.

Buying naked options means buying options without any protective trades to cover your investment if the underlying security moves against your expectations and hurts your trade.

Here is a typical example:

A trader strongly feels a particular stock will go up in the short term and assumes he can make a huge profit by buying a few call options and therefore goes ahead with the purchase. The trader knows if the underlying stock's price were to rise as expected, the potential upside on the profits would be unlimited, whereas, if it were to go down, the maximum loss would be curtailed to just the amount invested for purchasing the call options.

In theory, the trader's assumption is right and it may so happen that this one particular trade may pay off. However, in reality, it is equally possible the stock would not move as per expectations, or may even fall. If the latter happens, the call options' prices would start falling rapidly and may never recover thereby causing major losses to that trader.

It is almost impossible to predict the short-term movement of stock accurately every time and the trader who consistently keeps buying naked options hoping to get lucky is far more likely to lose much more than what he/she gains, in the long term.

For a person to make a profit after buying a naked option, the following things should fall in place:

1. The trader should predict the direction of the underlying stock's movement correctly.

2. The directional movement of the stock price should be quick enough so that the position can be closed before its gains get overrun by time-decay.

3. The rise in the option's premium price should also compensate for any potential drop in implied volatility from the time the option was purchased.

4. The trader should exit the trade at the right time before a reversal of the stock movement happens.

Needless to say, it is impractical to expect everything to fall in place simultaneously always and that is why naked-options traders often end up losing money even when they correctly guess the direction of the underlying stock's movement.

Having said all this, many such traders often think they would fare better the ensuing time after a botched trade and rinse and repeat their actions till they reach a point where they would have lost most of their capital and are forced to quit trading altogether.

My advice to you – never buy naked options (unless it is part of a larger strategy to hedge some position) because it's simply not worth the risk.

Note: While buying naked-options has only finite risk limited to the price of the premium paid, selling of naked-options has unlimited risk and has to be avoided too unless hedged properly.

2. Underestimating Time-Decay

A second major mistake of inexperienced traders is underestimating time-decay.

Time-decay is your worst enemy if you are the buyer of an option and you don't get a chance to exit your trade quickly enough.

If you are a call options buyer, you will notice that sometimes even when your underlying stock's price is increasing every day, your call option's price still doesn't rise or even falls. Alternately, if you are a put options buyer, you sometimes notice that your put option's price doesn't increase despite a fall in the price of the underlying stock. Both these situations can be confusing to somebody new to options trading.

The above problems occur when the rate of increase/decrease in the underlying stock's price is just not enough to outstrip the rate at which the option's time-value is eroding every day.

Therefore, any trading strategy deployed by an options trader should ideally have a method of countering/minimizing the effect of time-decay, or should make time-decay work in its favor, to ensure a profitable trade.

3. Buying Options with High Implied Volatility

Buying options in times of high volatility is yet another common mistake.

During times of high volatility, option premiums can get ridiculously overpriced and at such times, if an options trader buys options, even if the stock moves sharply in line with the trader's expectation, a large drop in the implied volatility would result in the option prices falling by a fair amount, resulting in losses to the buyer.

A particular situation I remember happened the day the results of the 'Brexit' referendum came through. The Nifty index reacting to the result (like most other global indices such as the Nasdaq 100) fell very sharply and the volatility index (VIX) jumped up by over 30%. The options premium for all Nifty options had become ludicrously high that day. However, this rise in volatility was only because of the market's knee-jerk reaction to an unexpected result and just a couple of days earlier, the market stabilized and started rising again; the VIX fell sharply and also brought down option premium prices accordingly.

Options traders who bought options at the time VIX was high would have realized their mistake a day or two earlier when the option prices came down causing them substantial losses because the volatility started to get back to normal figures.

4. Not Cutting Losses on Time

There is a famous saying among the folks on Wall Street - "Cut your losses short and let your winners run".

Even the most experienced options traders will make a bad trade once in a while. However, what differentiates them from a novice is that they know when to concede defeat and cut their losses. Amateurs hold on to losing trades in the hope they'll bounce back and eventually end up losing a larger chunk of their capital. The experienced traders, who know when to concede defeat, pull out early and re-invest the capital elsewhere.

Cutting losses in time is crucial especially when you trade a directional strategy and make a wrong call. The practical thing to do is to exit a losing position if it moves against expectation and erodes more than 2-3% of your total capital.

If you are a trader who strictly uses spread-based strategies, your losses will always be far more limited whenever you make a wrong call. Nevertheless, irrespective of the strategy used, when it becomes evident that the probability of profiting from trade is too less for whatsoever reason, it is prudent to cut losses and reinvest in a different position that has a greater chance of success rather than simply crossing your fingers or appealing to a higher power.

5. Keeping too many eggs in the same Basket

The experienced hands always know that once in a while, they will lose trade. They also know that they should never bet too much on a single trade which could considerably erode their capital were it to go wrong.

Professionals spread their risk across different trades and keep a maximum exposure of not more than 4-5% of their total available capital in a single trade for this very reason.

Therefore, if you have a total capital of $10,000, do not enter any single trade that has a risk of losing more than $500 in the worst-case scenario. Following such a practice will ensure the occasional loss is something you can absorb without seriously eroding your cash reserve. Fail to follow this rule and you may have the misfortune of seeing many months of profits wiped out by one losing trade.

6. Using Brokers who charge High Brokerages

A penny saved is a penny earned!

When I first entered the stock market many years ago, I didn't pay much attention to the brokerage I was paying. After all, the trading services I received were from one of the largest and most reputed banks in the country, and the brokerage charged by my provider wasn't very different from that of other banks that provided similar services.

Over the years, many discount brokerage firms started flourishing that charge considerably less, but I had not bothered changing my broker since I was used to the old one.

It was only when I quantified the differences that I realized having a low-cost broker made a huge difference.

If you are somebody who trades in the Indian Stock markets, check the table below for a quantified break-up of how brokerage charges can eat into your earnings over a year if you choose the wrong broker. The regular broker in the table below is the bank whose trading services I had been hitherto using and the discount broker is the one I use now. For the record, the former is also India's third-largest bank in the private sector and the latter is the most respected discount broker house in the country.

It is obvious from the table above that using a low-cost broker makes a huge difference especially when trading a strategy such as the Iron Condor (a relatively low-yield but high-probability strategy).

Also, it is not just the brokerage that burns a hole in your pocket; the annual maintenance fee is also higher for a regular broker and all these costs will make a huge difference in the long run.

Irrespective of which part of the world you trade from, always opt for a broker that provides the lowest possible brokerage because this will make a difference in the long term. Do a quantitative comparison using a table (something similar to the one I used above) and that would make it easier to decide who you should go with.

Note for India-based Traders: If you are a trader based in India or if you trade in the Indian Stock markets, I would strongly suggest using Zerodha, which has been consistently rated the best discount broker in the country. I have been using their services for the past couple of years and have found them to be particularly good. Their brokerage rates are among the best in the country, and on top of that, they provide excellent support when needed, and also maintain an exhaustive knowledge-base of articles. Lastly, their trading portal is very user friendly, and therefore, placing an order is quick and hassle-free.

Printed in the USA
CPSIA information can be obtained
at www.ICGtesting.com
LVHW052138121124
796473LV00039B/1048